TAILS OF THE UNEXPECTED

Amazing *but True* Stories of Cat
and Dog Escapades

COLLECTED BY

PATSY BLOOM

ILLUSTRATIONS BY RUSSELL JONES

GRUB STREET · LONDON

Published by Grub Street, The Basement, 10 Chivalry Road,
London SW11 1HT

Published in association with the Pet Plan Group

British Library Cataloguing in Publication Data

Tails of the Unexpected: True but Amazing Collection of Cat
and Dog Stories
I. Bloom, Patsy   II. Jones, Russell
636. 0887

ISBN   1-898697-28-0

Colour origination by Modern Age Repro, Hong Kong

Printed and bound in Italy

TAILS OF THE UNEXPECTED

Foreword

 I first had the idea for Pet Plan way back in 1976 when one of my dogs - Jamie - suffered a series of illnesses that required many visits to the vet and corresponding bills! These veterinary bills soon mounted up and when I came to pay them it hurt! I began then to realise that some kind of specialist insurance cover for animals seemed necessary.

After carrying out extensive research at veterinary surgeries and talking to pet owning friends, I became convinced that the idea was viable. In partnership with David Simpson - now Chairman of the Pet Plan Group - and with an investment of just £500, Pet Plan was born.

At the start it was meant to be just a hobby that earned a little extra pocket money. However the idea of health insurance for animals just took off. Pet Plan is now the leading animal health insurance specialist in the UK providing cover for over 350,000 dogs, cats and horses.

So, whether you own a pet or just share a love of cats and dogs, I hope that you will enjoy reading *Tails of the Unexpected* as much as I have enjoyed compiling it. It is truly amazing what dogs and cats get up to - both funny and heartbreaking - and this book contains just a tiny example of the stories we receive at Pet Plan.

The Pet Plan Group has always actively supported the veterinary profession and animal rescue organisations as I firmly believe it is a vital part of the Company's philosophy to put money back into animal welfare and help make a worthwhile investment into the long-term health and safety of animals.

In 1994 one of my dreams came true and the Pet Plan Charitable Trust was founded. This trust has been set up to provide grants for the welfare of dogs, cats and horses by funding clinical veterinary investigation, education and welfare projects and in 1995, I am delighted to say we were able to make the first of these annual awards to a selection of both scientific and welfare causes including the Pet Plan Cancer Care wing at the veterinary school of the University of Cambridge. The Royalties from the sale of this book will go to the Pet Plan Charitable Trust.

Finally, I would like to thank all the clients who made this book possible, Anne Dolamore for her enthusiasm and help in bringing the book to life and Russell Jones for his outstanding illustrations.

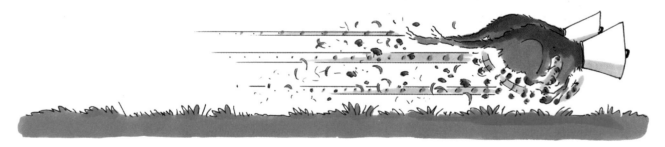

 PATSY BLOOM, Founder & Chief Executive, Pet Plan Group.

Totally Toothless

NAME	Marco
AGE	10 years
BREED	Yorkshire Terrier
OWNER	Mr & Mrs J Simpson

Marco the Yorkie wasn't much good at tricks.
In the past, his owners had secretly hoped that as he'd grown older
he might have mastered the art of leaping through fiery hoops, but this was not to be.
Even the simple tasks of sitting and staying on command seemed totally beyond the dog.
However, there was one party piece that he did very well. Marco could smile. A polite request
for him to 'show his pearlies' was all the prompting he needed to beam forth a dazzlingly toothy
grin from ear to ear.

But sadly for the dog, not only could he smile very well, he could
also eat chocolate like there was no tomorrow and over
the years his weakness for Black Magic and Milk Tray
took its toll on his once flawless choppers. Inevitably
the day came when his vet was forced to remove
them, leaving Marco with two rows of shining gums
of which he was, and still is, very proud!

Marco continues to smile at every opportunity but his owner reports that it's now not
nearly as pretty a sight as it used to be.

Blitzed

Since mayhem and devastation seemed to follow him around, Blitz had been very aptly named by his family. One of his more destructive attacks was cleverly timed to coincide with the 50th Anniversary of the air raids on Coventry and it involved extensive property damage and two innocent civilian casualties.

Having left the dog alone one Sunday for a couple of hours, his owners returned to base to find their three-piece suite had been magically transformed into a forty-one piece, the coffee table and standard lamp had been chewed to matchwood and worst of all, in the middle of the wreckage lay the broken, lifeless bodies of the family budgie and the pet goldfish, the latter's bowl shattered and its ornamental seaweed eaten!

The dog's owners were not at all happy with Blitz but knowledge that their insurance policy would cover the damage took the edge off their displeasure.

Blitz died last year, shot down in his prime. He was long ago forgiven for his sins and is sadly missed by his family who report that with no dog and hardly any furniture the house now seems so empty.

NAME	Blitz
AGE	5 years
BREED	German Shepherd Dog
OWNER	Kerry Sides

Russian Treasure Trove

LOOKS LIKE BREAKFAST TO ME!

Vladimir developed a taste for the good things in life at a very early age. By the time he was two he'd eaten several pairs of shoes and sun-glasses, countless items of mail and enough bank notes to reduce his family to tears. His favourite snack however was a medium to rare collar, particularly if he was wearing it at the time!

No one knew or could guess how Vladimir managed to get the thing off his neck and into his stomach but speculation as to the un-dog-like contortions involved challenged the most vivid of veterinary imaginations for many months.

Rumour has it that while Vlad was being treated at the local practice, a member of staff, whose true vocation was scrap dealing, made a sizeable second income by hoarding the countless buckles, rivets and studs salvaged from the dog's stomach over the years.

NAME	Vladimir
AGE	3 years
BREED	Labrador
OWNER	Mrs Sylvie Pierre

Tanks for the Fish

Jake's life changed dramatically the day he caught his first heady whiff of fish food. After wolfing down an entire tub of the stuff carelessly spilt by his owner, he knew he would never again be content with the common or garden goo-in-a-tin and dried hard tack that had up until then been his staple diet. Fish flakes were the business!

After that first taste, the cat stationed himself permanently by the fish tank threatening the inmates and his owner with violence if he wasn't fed from the tub on a regular basis and on the odd occasion when a meal was late, he showed his displeasure by making a loud, irritating noise similar to a triggered smoke alarm. Since Jake liked nothing better than to eat at three o'clock in the morning, this phenomenon led to many rude awakenings and sleepless nights for his family.

NAME	Jake
AGE	19 months
BREED	Domestic Long-Haired Cat
OWNER	Mrs B W Dunn

Barking Mad

It's surprising how much damage a loud, unexpected bark from a very large dog can inflict on a very small one as Rocky, a King Charles Spaniel found out one day. He ended up with extensive injuries after being knocked for six in just such an incident.

Eye witnesses reported that the sudden bark from deep within a huge, unidentified beast standing next to Rocky outside a supermarket must have registered at least 9.6 on the Richter Scale and it all but put the little dog into orbit!

Landing without a parachute was never going to be easy for him but apart from a fractured elbow and a hardly noticeable but permanent limp, Rocky has made a complete recovery.

........Charlie the 9-month-old English Bull Terrier once swallowed a large towel which necessitated surgery and hospitalization for 3 days and a bill for £696.........

NAME	Rocky
AGE	4 years
BREED	Cavalier King Charles Spaniel
OWNER	Miss B Webster
AMOUNT CLAIMED	£996.77 (Total claims to do with leg fracture!)

WOOF!

Dane on the Rampage

When Sheba made up her mind it was time to go home, she meant business and since she weighed only slightly less than a small hippo, nothing was going to stop her!

Tied to an advertising sign outside her local supermarket one morning she decided that shopping was not quite her thing and with one mighty tug she tore the sign from its foundation and dragging it along in her wake, made for home sweet home as fast as a Great Dane could gallop.

The trail of destruction she ploughed along her route would not have looked out of place in Beirut and later, when an angry mob turned up at her front door, clamouring to be compensated for wrecked vehicles, Sheba's owners were grateful beyond words for their third party insurance.

NAME	Sheba
AGE	7 years
BREED	Great Dane
OWNER	G A & S P Budd

Useless 'n' Plonker

At six months old the world can look a daunting place for two very small Retriever pups. Plonker and Useless, two such mini beasts, regarded a flight of stone steps joining two levels of the back garden as their personal Mt. Everest and one afternoon set out from base camp to scale the north face.

It took an hour to reach the summit where, from the dizzy altitude of fifteen feet they looked down onto the neat lawn and flower beds below and became frozen with fear! It was obvious that getting down was going to be much more hassle than getting up!

After ten minutes of indecision, Plonker was the first to see a solution. He head butted his brother off the summit, sending him in the fastest possible way to the bottom for help. Useless suffered multiple bruising and broken teeth.

Plonker had the good sense to wait patiently and was air lifted to safety a few minutes later by his owner.

NAME	Useless & Plonker
AGE	At time of story 6 months, now 5 years
BREED	Flatcoat Retrievers
OWNER	Dr A D Brown

Suffering Snakes

Roxy, a Staffordshire Bull Terrier, managed one morning to turn a peaceful stretch of Surrey heathland into something resembling a scene from 'Jungle Book'.

NAME	Roxy
AGE	4 years
BREED	Staffordshire Bull Terrier
OWNER	Alex Copland

Poking his nose into a tuft of grass, the dog disturbed a sleeping adder and within seconds the beasts were locked in combat. The battle didn't last long. One bite and it was all over. The snake slid off into the scrub, Roxy collapsed in shock and his owners, realizing what had happened began discussing who would play John Wayne and suck out the poison!

Since neither of them fancied the short straw, they carried Roxy several hundred yards to the car and rushed him to the local vet. There was no serum available at the surgery, so just the symptoms were treated and apart from having to hobble around for a couple of days on a leg swollen to four times its usual size, the Staffie made a full recovery.

A VET'S STORY

Panty Passion

Described by her owners as a mog with a fuller figure, Kiri, a very fat black and grey Persian had the embarrassing habit of stealing items of underwear from around the house and dragging them from room to room in a lewd and suggestive manner. During her routine she'd also deafen the family with a highly pitched, highly irritating shriek.

A visit to the surgery confirmed that the profession in general is baffled by this common feline fixation for lace undies but in an effort to arrive at a diagnosis for her anxious clients, the vet brought all her medical skill and knowledge to bear on the situation. She suggested that Kiri may have been a stripper in an earlier life!

Well, that's showbiz!

........*Jasper's owners have a family of birds which nest above the bedroom window each year. This year the young British Blue tried to make 'friends' with them and fell out of the bedroom window after managing to squeeze through a window gap normally reserved, or so his owners say, for a mouse. Jasper suffered a fractured back leg.........*

NAME | Kiri
AGE | 3 years
BREED | Persian Cat
OWNER | Susan Pease

Karda's Fashion Statement

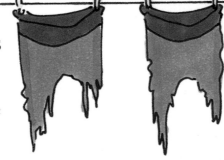

Karda the Retriever was another clothes fancier, but rather than drag his bits and pieces of swag around the house, he preferred to eat it!

As various items of clothing disappeared over a period of months, his owner became very concerned, especially as he seemed to be ending up with more odd socks than a launderette proprietor.

Things came to a head one day when Karda was violently sick on the carpet and a visit to the vet revealed a complete pair of nylon tights tangled up in his intestines!

NAME	Karda
AGE	4 years
BREED	Flatcoat Retriever
OWNER	Mrs K Moore

Weekend Break

NAME	Tessie
AGE	4 years
BREED	Unknown
OWNER	Mrs A Stait

Considering Tessie had been rescued after being thrown from a car on a busy main road, she'd ended up with little or no emotional scarring. However, there was one minor quirk in the dog's character of which her new owners quickly became aware. When they took her on a weekend break to a holiday hotel, they found out that Tessie didn't like being alone.

Leaving the dog asleep in their suite as they went down to dinner, they returned to find that what had once been a five star room had been reduced in stature to 'basic accommodation'! The carpet was shredded, the door had been stripped of paint, the wallpaper was in tatters and most of the antique furniture had been remodeled along minimalist lines.

Happily, Tessie's owners were fully insured but they still have occasional nightmares about a mega hotel bill being handed over by a smiling but sinister receptionist and often wake up screaming in the middle of the night!

Zak the Prof

As a breed, Boxers are not especially known for their dynamic I.Q., but Zak's family were quite prepared to swear that their dog was not only bright but that he sat at the very pinnacle of the canine intellectual heap. They were convinced he could read!

Having left him alone to protect the presents under the tree one Christmas Eve, the family returned to find that Zak had opened half a dozen packages before the big day, amazingly all of them addressed to him personally! Others, even some containing chocolates, usually irresistible Boxer food, were left untouched.

His family were so impressed by this wondrous feat that they considered chipping-in to buy the dog an extra present - a year's subscription to the *Sunday Telegraph!*

NAME	Zak
AGE	3 years
BREED	Boxer
OWNER	Brenda Stones

'Ere and Now

NAME	Sophie
AGE	10 ½ years
BREED	English Springer Spaniel
OWNER	Mrs Lynne J Kerr

Sophie, a nine-year-old Springer Spaniel gave a whole new meaning to the medical term 'glue ear' when an elderly member of her family skilfully administered a shot of super glue into her shell-like in mistake for ear drops!

An urgent trip to the vet was needed to free Sophie from a very sticky situation but thankfully she was none the worse for her experience. Now, by way of reprisal, the dog chooses to be selectively stone deaf to any requests or commands and only responds to the words 'grub-up' and 'walkies'.

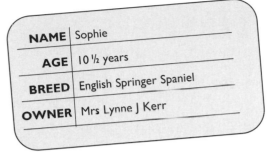

Hic....

Dan the Spaniel lived to regret the Christmas Eve he pinched a family-size box of real rum truffles and downed the lot in one go. The immediate feeling was one of canine euphoria as he staggered around the house howling his way through a few favourite tunes but sadly the hangover that followed a few hours later was monumental and required a visit to the surgery.

The vet was tempted to prescribe the 'hair of the dog' but instead suggested plenty of quiet and a good night's sleep.

Dan still pinches chocolates but now he always checks for the unmistakable aroma of alcohol before he downs his spoils.

NAME	Dan
AGE	11 years
BREED	Cocker Spaniel
OWNER	Mike Tregenza

A VET'S STORY) *Deadly Ambush*

A call from the zoo to its local veterinary practice one afternoon threw the surgery into total chaos. There had been a fracas in the tiger compound and one of their cats would be arriving shortly with a keeper for emergency repairs.

As the practice geared up to receive a huge, snarling beast in a steel cage, the keeper strolled in with a small ginger tom in a cardboard box!

In search of a square meal the moggy had wandered into the tiger compound and straight into an ambush set by one of the more irritable inmates. The spectacle that followed reminded onlookers of one of the more harrowing scenes from 'Life and Death on the Serengeti' but after a brief but bloody struggle the moggy was able to leg it to safety.

He ended up with only three toes on one foot but a great story to tell his grandkittens!

That Champagne Moment

Not only had Bellman been born with the standard issue Bloodhound features of a mega-large nose and a seriously pucker sense of smell, he'd also been blessed with the ability to swallow and pass through his system almost anything he fancied.

Sitting around one evening at a Christmas party minding his own business, the dog was alerted by a loud popping sound as a family member broke open a bottle of 'bubbly'. Eye-witnesses reported that the cork shot across the room at somewhere near the speed of sound towards Bellman who, totally out of character for such an ungainly hound, dived athletically across the carpet to catch and swallow the missile in one gulp!

Although a trip to the vet was considered in order, fears for Bellman's safety were quickly dispelled by his owners who detailed the dog's legendary swallowing abilities. Objects that had already passed through his system with no problem included a Tesco shopping bag, a pair of panties and a large plastic knob from a slow cooker! Depositing the champagne cork on the front lawn the following day, complete with wire cage, also proved no problem for a dog with Bellman's talents!

NAME	Bellman
AGE	7½ years
BREED	Bloodhound
OWNER	Miss J E Corner

Marksman on Target

Prior to the 'Great Storm' of 1987, a greenhouse stood intact in Marksman's garden. At the end of a hawthorn hedge, it separated him from his great pal and next door neighbour, Ben the Corgi. When the storm obligingly blew out the glass leaving just the frame, it proved no obstacle to an athletic Beagle and Marksman would bound through several times a day to play with his mate.

A few weeks later, reglazing commenced with Marksman being kept out of the way so the contractors could work in peace.

The following day, with the Beagle once more loose in the garden, his owners were horrified to see him begin a lengthy run up towards the greenhouse, obviously unaware that the glass had been replaced.

Before they could stop him, Marksman had taken off like a pole vaulter and crashed his way through to next door's garden in a shower of glass and tomato plants!

The dog ended up with twenty-six stitches in a chest wound and his owner's insurance company with a large bill for reglazing!

NAME | Marksman
AGE | 9 ¾ years
BREED | Beagle
OWNER | Jackie Mullis

Magic Mushrooms

Delf's owner reasoned that if a pig could be taught to find truffles, then his dog, a Labrador and a very bright spark to boot, could be taught to find mushrooms.

The training was successful and all went well until one day on the way home from a hunt, Delf became suddenly quiet and withdrawn. A few minutes later things went rapidly downhill and she began rolling her eyes from side to side and foaming at the mouth.

NAME	Delf
AGE	14 years
BREED	Labrador
OWNER	Mr K Easton

One look at her glazed and vacant expression told her owner that the dog's mind had embarked on some sort of cosmic journey so he rushed her to the local surgery. The vet treated her with a dose of washing soda and after much heaving and retching Delf deposited a neat pile of toadstools onto the surgery floor. Shortly afterwards she arrived back on planet earth.

Delf still hunts mushrooms but being intelligent, she now knows the difference between the ones you put in an omelette and the ones that put you into orbit, but her owner always carries a dose of washing soda, just in case!

A VET'S STORY

Wet Wet Wet

It's
a fact of
life that cats
and water don't mix, but a
veterinary practice reported last year that one of
their patients, a small tabby kitten, loved to take a nap
half in and half out of his water bowl during hot weather.

The moggy's owners assured the staff that they took it in turns to retrieve the
kitten from the bowl so that he could be wrung out every now and then to prevent his
lower half becoming waterlogged!

The Miracle Cure

NAME	Toby (Blazing Starlight)
AGE	4 years
BREED	German Shepherd Dog
OWNER	Bernard Mason

For three months, Toby suffered from severe dermatitis. He was tested for over fifty different allergies and prescribed everything from oil of evening primrose capsules to antihistamine tablets. In spite of all the treatments, the condition worsened rapidly until Toby seemed to consist of more dermatitis than dog!

Following a last ditch phone call to a specialist, steroids were prescribed and these were to be picked up the following day. But during the night Toby's condition miraculously returned to normal.

It was some days later that his owner discovered a card containing an entire month's supply of birth control pills which Toby had obviously pinched and eaten.

He's now claiming a brand new cure for canine dermatitis!

Ten Inches of Trouble

Sapphire had a huge appetite for anything and everything so long as it bore no resemblance to food. Curiously, she seemed much more attracted to the garden gate and the bedroom carpet than to a tasty pile of meaty chunks in gravy. Hence she was very underweight.

One day in the garden she set about dining out on what can only be described as a log. It was almost twelve inches in length and sadly, Sapphire could only manage ten of these before it dawned on her that she had bitten off much more than she could chew.

The 'log' was retrieved by a team of surgeons. It was trapped somewhere between her throat and tummy and removed in a complicated operation.

Apart from making a meal of her drip tubing, the dog made a trouble-free recovery and her owners report that the experience seems to have given Sapphire a taste for real dog food and she's now a well-rounded winner of local dog shows.

NAME	Sapphire
AGE	I year
BREED	Pointer
OWNER	Mrs J Drake

Hole in One

Kurt, in common with most dogs, would rather suffer a severe bout of kennel cough than endure the horrors and indignity of the nose drops that prevent it!

The practice where he was due to undergo the ordeal was being remodeled and a temporary false wall had been erected between the surgery and waiting room.

The owner's elderly father held Kurt on the table but as the vet advanced menacingly towards his hooter, it all became too much for the dog. With one giant leap, he was off the table and dragging his minder with him, he crashed through the false wall, shot through the crowded waiting room and made for the hills, his handler still in tow!

........*Jack the Birman decided to join in the Christmas festivities and helped himself to a piece of Dundee cake on the quiet. He subsequently became very ill and was taken to the vet who operated on a blocked intestine. The cause of the problem turned out to be an almond from the top of the cake.........!*

NAME | Kurt
AGE | 10 years
BREED | German Shepherd Dog
OWNER | Karen Bloomfield

Eko the Stunt Cat

Eko was a hard act to follow. Most days in summer she'd walk a narrow ledge twenty-five feet above the garden to sun herself on a neighbour's roof.

One morning her owner called 'grub up' when the cat was halfway across the ledge and before she could choose between personal safety and a square meal, Eko had lost her balance and together with a dislodged potted plant, had nosedived the twenty-five feet into a thorn bush!

The plant was killed instantly but Eko survived with multiple bruising and a lot of thorns in strategic parts of her anatomy.

Happily she made a complete recovery but her owner reports that the prickly experience hasn't blunted the cat's high wire act. One down, eight to go!

NAME	Eko
AGE	1 year
BREED	Tortoiseshell Cat
OWNER	Lisa M St John

Blow Out

Molly was a little dog with a big appetite and one of her regular snacking stops around the house was the kitchen waste-bin with all its left-over goodies. Following one bout of scavenging, her behaviour became very erratic and she started to suffer muscle spasms.

The unlikely cause of her condition turned out to be a quantity of plastic explosive that had stuck to wrappers discarded in the bin by a young family member who was in the army cadet force. Molly had eaten the T.N.T in mistake for chocolate!

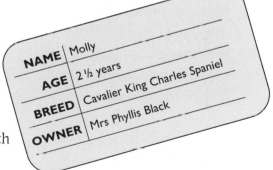

All naked flames in the house were extinguished, (in case Molly passed wind) and she was rushed to the vet where she underwent three days of unpleasant treatment.

The dog made a complete recovery but now hates visiting the local practice. Her owner reports that she's had words with Molly and warned her that if she gives any trouble in future she'll be pointed in the direction of the surgery, the blue touch paper will be lit and the family will retire to a safe distance!

NAME	Molly
AGE	2 ½ years
BREED	Cavalier King Charles Spaniel
OWNER	Mrs Phyllis Black

Bobby's Big Nite Out

Bobby was an old hand at riding the buses and always became excited at the prospect of his weekly trip to town.

One evening out walking with his owner, the sight of a double decker on the opposite side of the road, lights ablaze and engine throbbing was all too much for the dog and before he could be stopped, he'd bounded onto the bus, taken the stairs in one bound and had made himself comfortable on the front seat! As the bus pulled away and disappeared down the road, Bobby's horrified owner swears she saw the dog smile and wave at her.

In spite of phone calls to the bus company and desperate radio messages between drivers, the wanderer was nowhere to be found and his deeply depressed owner returned home convinced that she had seen the last of him.

However there was no need to worry as the dog was waiting for her at the garden gate when she arrived half an hour later. It was probably the thought of missing out on two square meals a day that had worried Bobby into jumping ship at the first stop.

NAME	Bobby
AGE	20 months
BREED	German Shepherd Dog
OWNER	Miss Eleanor Chan

Street Fightin' Cat

Bruno, a tough-as-old-leather tabby, had lived rough on the mean streets of London most of his life and he had the scar tissue to prove it. However, when he was rescued by new owners and taken to live in the peace and quiet of the country he was to find out quickly that he had jumped straight out of the frying pan into a red hot fire.

Bruno was forced to wage war with everything on four legs to carve out a patch of territory for himself. Apart from an army of country cousins who specialized in grievous bodily harm, he had to do battle with badgers, huge rats with black belts in karate, foxes and mean-minded farmyard dogs who didn't believe in taking prisoners!

NAME	Bruno
AGE	12 years
BREED	Tabby
OWNER	Mrs M J Lanning

After eight years of continuous jungle warfare and countless trips to the local surgery to have his combat wounds stitched, his owners report that at last Bruno has a patch of his own and, dangling from his flea collar, a conspicuous gallantry medal awarded by his admiring vet.

Easter Aches

Since being rescued from an owner who had neglected and starved her, Jade had developed a tremendous interest in food. Her new family described her as having the capacity of a builder's skip with a Gannet's enthusiasm to fill it.

One Easter the dog was carelessly left alone for half an hour with sixteen large chocolate eggs belonging to the children. It was all the time Jade needed to finish the lot along with the cardboard packaging and silver paper. The family returned to find her belly-up on the carpet in obvious and very serious post-nosh trouble.

NAME	Jade
AGE	8 years
BREED	Labrador Cross
OWNER	Mrs A Poll

Jade needed a stomach wash and was kept at the local surgery for two days of observation. She recovered well but by all accounts the experience has failed to cure her and she's still a chocaholic. Worst of all the children still haven't forgiven her!

A VET'S STORY

Not So Pretty Polly

Polly, a four-year-old domestic mog and Duncan Goodhew the famous amphibian, shared something in common - they both suffered from a severe shortage of hair!

When her coat suddenly started to thin, Polly became severely traumatized by her appearance and after much testing at the local surgery, it was found she was allergic to flea bites.

Her vet waged chemical warfare on the little blighters and in no time at all the uninvited guests had been evicted and Polly's coat had returned to normal. Sadly, the same treatment will not work for Mr. Goodhew!

Snowbound

The snow
in the garden
was five inches
deep as Melissa the
Pekinese strode towards the dog flap and growled
'I'm just stepping outside - I may be some time'.

When she failed to return after half an hour, a posse was mustered and
sent out to follow her paw prints in the snow. They led to a large ornamental

fishpond hidden by trees where the leader of the search party spotted a small wet nose just above the surface of the freezing water. Melissa had obviously fallen in and more used to lying on a warm lap than an arctic ice flow, had not had the strength to haul herself out!

The dog was rescued, rushed indoors and warmed with hot towels on the vet's instruction. It was some time before Melissa's teeth stopped chattering but happily she made a full recovery from her arctic ordeal.

NAME	Melissa
AGE	8 years
BREED	Pekinese
OWNER	George F Johnson

Brief Encounter

Ben the Retriever had looked a bit down in the dumps and an x-ray at the local surgery showed a large obstruction in his stomach. He was operated on the same day and to everyone's amazement, a complete pair of M&S Y-fronts was removed from his interior.

The surgeon reckoned a trip to the launderette would see them as good as new but Ben's owner preferred to bin them and dine out on the story.

NAME	Ben
AGE	2 years
BREED	Golden Retriever
OWNER	Mrs J E Parkin

........Wispa was a 2-year-old Chocolate Burmese when a radiator fell on her that had been left leaning against a wall by the plumber. The painful result was a broken hind leg.........

Cheeky's Luck Runs Out

Cheeky had all nine lives intact up until the day he was rescued and taken to live with a new family.

No sooner had he ventured through the cat flap than he was in collision with a car which broke his jaw and left him severely concussed. Before the bone had mended, he was involved in another road accident, this time a rear end shunt that required partial amputation of his tail.

By now the cat was exhausted but fate had not finished with him yet. A few days later he was successfully targeted by an unknown urban gunslinger and peppered with lead shot before he could take cover.

As he lay on the operating table, the cat must have hoped that his ordeal was now over but his owner had decided to kill two birds with one stone. Since Cheeky was already at the surgery she decided it was as good a time as any to have him neutered!

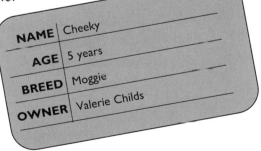

NAME	Cheeky
AGE	5 years
BREED	Moggie
OWNER	Valerie Childs

Everyone hopes Cheeky's run of bad luck will now change and that the rest of his life will pass without incident. Watch this space!

Ollie's Technicolour Yawn

Oliver is a second-hand dog in the strictest sense of the term as he was found curled up amongst the clapped out furniture and useless bits and pieces at a car boot sale! He was rescued on the spot and taken to a new home where, on the following bank holiday, his new owner looked into the garden and was horrified to see him half way through a box of slug pellets.

Over the phone the vet instructed a dose of washing soda to induce vomiting which Oliver's owner followed with her own special mixture to neutralize the poison.

What happened next was spectacular, as a pint of milk, 3 raw eggs, half a bottle of cooking oil and two dozen lime green slug pellets shot through the air to land fifteen feet away on the living room carpet, changing it from plain to patterned in an instant! Oliver made a complete recovery. Unfortunately the carpet didn't.

........*A St Bernard called Wolfgang was out for an early morning walk along the clifftops of North Devon when he lost his footing and fell 200 feet onto the beach below. The 2-year-old survived to claim £1,276*........

NAME	Oliver
AGE	8 years
BREED	Collie Cross
OWNER	J A Lodge

Live Wire

A lady arrived at a surgery one evening with a very large, very wet mongrel. She'd been relaxing in the garden, enjoying the sun when the beast had suddenly been catapulted over the hedge that separated her land from a railway line and deposited head first into her small fishpond! The unfortunate mutt had evidently stood on a live rail and had been boosted into orbit courtesy of Network South East.

The dog was examined and pronounced fit though a bit shocked by the episode. However, the staff agreed that his new hairdo was a complete disaster!

A VET'S STORY

Fangs for the Memory

A vet was called out one evening to catch a feral cat who had been described by the elderly lady in whose garden shed the animal had been trapped, as having all the charm of a serial killer on steroids!

When the vet arrived he was pushed inside the shed with the words 'he's in there somewhere' and the door was slammed firmly behind him. As his eyes were adjusting to the dim light a snarling mass of teeth and claws flew past his face almost doing a Vincent Van Gogh on his ear as it went!

As the cat turned and leapt for a second attack, the vet, remembering that his practice was at the cutting edge of high-tech medicine, took a giant stride forward in the field of veterinary anaesthesia and promptly subdued the animal with a large plank of wood!

Thankfully the vet knew what he was about and the serial killer made a complete recovery.

A Turn of the Screw

Following complications after a road accident, Sam the Retriever needed major surgery to realign the joints in his legs. This involved attaching an elaborate arrangement of ironwork to the dog in the middle of which was a nut. This was to be tightened 1 mm every day with a spanner wielded by Sam's owner.

The kitchen where this procedure was carried out resembled a scene from the Spanish Inquisition, but the dog was a great patient and within no time his joints had been stretched, the ironwork dismantled and Sam was back on his elongated pins.

NAME	Sam
AGE	3 years
BREED	Golden Retriever
OWNER	Mrs J Skoulding

Ramraiding Rottweiler

Otto the Rottie was not at the front of the queue when brains were being allocated, and this was clearly demonstrated one afternoon during a country walk.

It seems that for reasons known only to Otto, he suddenly about-turned on the bridle path along which he was travelling, charged off in a cloud of dust and headbutted a brand new 4 x 4 Jeep that was following along behind.

There was extensive damage to the side of the vehicle but a later examination at a surgery showed Otto's skull, and the tiny brain it contained, to be completely free of damage!

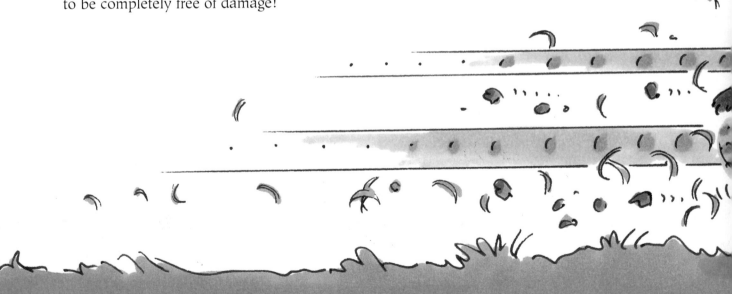

NAME	Otto
AGE	6 years
BREED	Rottweiler
OWNER	Lorraine Trimby

A VET'S STORY

Open Wide

A vet from Shropshire was called out one morning to look at a lame horse. On completion of the examination, the owner asked if he could check out her cat who had been off colour. The vet examined the moggy, prescribed some pills and trundelled off, leaving behind a set of hoof-testers he'd used to examine the horse.

On his return a week later to check his patients, the vet was stunned to hear the lady complain about the difficulty she'd had administering the cat's pills with the contraption he'd left behind!

The moggy is still undergoing treatment for post traumatic stress syndrome.

Whoops a Daisy

NAME	Daisy
AGE	3½ years
BREED	English Bull Terrier
OWNER	P D Monk

Unless judged by a real fan, the English Bull Terrier has always been about as far away from the canine brains n' beauty premier league as a dog can get and Daisy, a Cornish member of the breed was no exception.

Her owner assessed the dog's I.Q. as being only marginally superior to that of a tin of brewer's yeast and one of the main manifestations of her simple mindedness seemed to be her complete inability to spot the difference between food and rubbish.

Over the years Daisy has kept her vet on the gravy train with countless visits to the surgery to have mountains of indigestible garbage removed from her interior. Her family has come to refer to these visits as trips to the plumber for a touch of Dyno-Rodding!

Since terminal dimness is incurable, the vet expects no improvement in Daisy's condition.

A Stitch in Time

If synchronized swimming ever becomes a recognized event at canine obedience competitions then Bruno the Springer will be a certain gold medallist.

Out walking near a lake one day with his owner, Bruno spotted a brace of ducks with a gaggle of young un's in tow come steaming over the horizon. Launching himself into the water via a triple somersault with tuck, Bruno gave chase and for the next hour followed the fluffy armada around the lake perimeter, the ducks always managing to stay ahead by a short nose.

After a marathon swim which left him totally waterlogged, Bruno crawled out of the lake too exhausted to ease himself safely over a barbed wire fence. The resulting injuries to his reproductive equipment brought tears to the eyes of the local vet but after Bruno had been wrung out, stitched up and rested, he was as good as new.

NAME	Bruno
AGE	3 years
BREED	English Springer Spaniel
OWNER	Mrs Beryl Monck

........Trampas the Rhodesian Ridgeback became seriously ill with bone marrow failure which required daily blood tests for 3 weeks and an urgent blood transfusion from his sister Shanty. He never needed sedation or restraint of any kind and because he was so brave he was given a champagne party by his veterinary surgeon and nurses on his discharge.........

Digging for Victory

When Thor moved into a new ground floor flat it was made clear from the outset that the indoor area belonged to his owner and the back garden belonged to him.

This arrangement worked well until it was decided to build a patio on Thor's patch and the dog suddenly developed a passion for civil engineering.

Tunnelling was Thor's speciality and if a section of the patio that infringed upon his territory had not collapsed in on him one evening, he'd probably be well on his way to France by now!

The accident sparked a major rescue and the dog required eight stitches in a damaged paw and treatment for shock. His owner reports that since the disaster, Thor has lost interest in tunnelling and is now acting as consultant to a gang of men building a kitchen extension.

NAME	Thor
AGE	15 months
BREED	Weimeraner
OWNER	Miss D Blake

........*Little Zoe the Cocker Spaniel was being walked by her owner when she spotted another dog coming in the opposite direction. Dogs will be dogs - and Zoe decided to go and make friends. She raced off, still attached to her extending lead which she managed to wrap around an elderly lady. The woman was tripped up resulting in a broken wrist and received compensation and costs to the tune of £666* ....

Back from the Brink

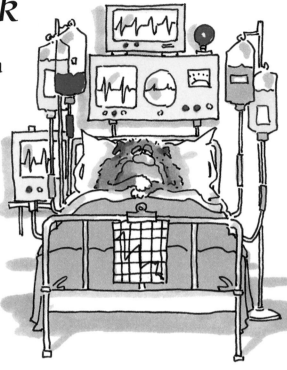

Winston needed all the stiff upper lip a Bulldog could muster to see him through a mystery illness so severe in its intensity it would probably have felled a fully grown Hippo.

Within a very short time of feeling under the weather one morning, the dog suddenly found himself on the table, wired to a drip and well within field goal range of the pearly gates. As a team of vets hovered above him, thrashing about for a diagnosis, Winston began rejecting all his main organs and severe haemorrhaging started throughout his body. As if this weren't enough, it was also thought he was going blind.

After a day of being tested without result for every condition in the manual of veterinary nasties, Winston's liver and kidneys were on the point of complete collapse and as his temperature soared off the chart, everyone waited for the inevitable. However, just as the last rites were about to be read the dog began a miraculous recovery and within a few days he was up on his paws and back to the old wheezing and slobbering routine that's such a hallmark of the breed.

Winston's vet, still baffled by the miracle, puts it all down to the Bulldog spirit!

NAME	Winston
AGE	3½ years
BREED	Bulldog
OWNER	Mrs Janis Dell

A VET'S STORY

Condomania

A very sheepish looking chap brought his mog into a busy practice one morning. He confessed that the cat may have eaten a condom and on being pressed for the whole story, added that it was a used one.

Amidst much sniggering amongst the staff, the mog was admitted for observation to give Mother Nature time to take her course. This she fortunately did the following day.

By way of consolation and to help the embarrassed man look on the bright side, one wag at the surgery suggested that at least he could be grateful the condom had been removed from its position before the cat decided to sink his teeth in!

Boneshaker

Whiskey had a reputation for involving herself in incredibly stupid accidents, one of the most bizarre of which happened over Christmas when she managed to wedge her bottom jaw firmly into the hollow of a marrow bone.

It took a surgeon half an hour of careful sawing before the bone could be dislodged and another half to check Whiskey over before she was free to return home to find even more sillier things to do.

NAME	Whiskey
AGE	1 year
BREED	Greyhound
OWNER	Mrs M Young

A VET'S STORY

Calorie-Controlled Kitty

There are thin cats and fat cats in this world but Matty the ginger tom was a cat of Cyril Smith proportions. His condition was caused purely and simply by eating huge quantities of food and as he waddled into the surgery one day with all the grace of a Sumo wrestler, he caused quite a stir amongst the staff. Weighing in at almost 9 kg, it was clear to the vet that a stringent calorie-controlled diet was the answer to Matty's problems.

A regime that would have made a weight watcher shudder was introduced and it didn't take long for it to work its magic. Within a couple of weeks Matty saw his feet for the first time since kittenhood and a month later, with his life of gluttony firmly behind him, he'd become a slim young tom about town!

Turbo Goes Bonkers

Ben and Toby, aka Bonkers and Turbo, were as alike as two peas in a pod. They prided themselves on a relationship built on equality and fraternity and all went well until one day Ben was fitted with a cone collar to protect a row of stitches in his chin. Toby became insanely jealous of his mate's new acquisition and began taking every opportunity to wrestle the collar off his neck.

In the interests of Ben's general health and the well-being of his chin, the dogs' owner returned to the surgery where the vet came up with the perfect solution. She fitted Toby with an identical collar and the problem was solved in a jiffy.

The sight of two Bassets tearing about the local park like jet propelled megaphones was a sight still remembered by the locals!

NAME	Ben and Toby
AGE	5 & 6 years
BREED	Basset Hounds
OWNER	Mrs Bronwen Green

........*When the milklady came to collect her money, for some unknown reason, Tippy, a 7-year-old Border Collie, rushed out and nipped the milklady on her leg dramatically increasing the milk bill by a further £5000 in compensation........*

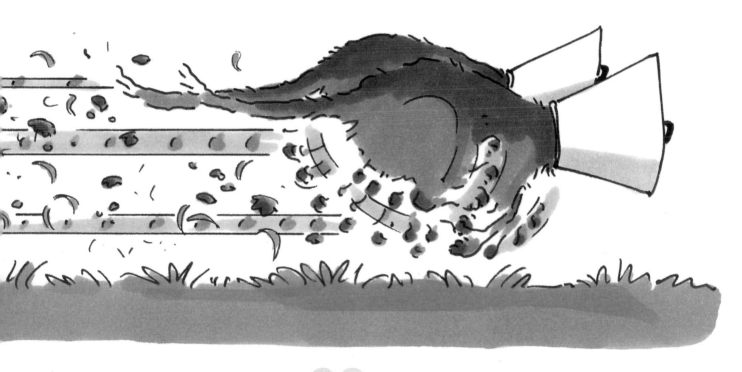

Sick 'n Single

Perhaps because Duke had been born deaf, his sense of smell had developed to Bloodhound standards and his owners were constantly amazed at his ability to sniff out anything edible; even up-wind at two hundred paces.

One bonfire night, six pounds of onions had been cooked at a fireworks party to add to barbecue hot dogs but before they could end up in the guests, they ended up in Duke who had sniffed 'em out and finished them off before the cook could get to them.

An overdose of onions can damage red blood cells and Duke was a very sick dog for a week. He was also a very lonely mutt as his family and friends found his smelly breath made him totally unkissable!

NAME	Duke
AGE	4 years
BREED	Dalmatian
OWNER	Mrs L A Cecil

A VET'S STORY

Floored by a Fish

Katy's owner was a big fan of tropical fish and kept a collection in a large aquarium in the lounge. Her moggy showed great interest in a nine-inch-long catfish that lived at the bottom of the tank and over the months they eyed each other in a 'cold war' sort of way through the glass for long periods of time.

One day curiosity finally got the better of the cat and she dunked a paw into the deep in an effort to eject the fish. Sadly for her, the enemy was a distant cousin to a Great White Shark and it attacked with all the venom of a man eater, sending Katy flying through the cat-flap not to be seen again for twenty-four hours!

She now observes the newly named 'Jaws' from a very safe distance.

Tall Tail?

A cat was admitted to a surgery in the West Midlands for treatment to his tail following a road accident.

To everyone's amazement, an x-ray revealed that the tail had been elongated by precisely the same width as a Dunlop 195/65 radial tyre and the stretched portion contained no bones whatsoever.

The entire tail had to be amputated but the mog made a full recovery.

........Ember, a 7-year-old Newfoundland, swallowed a whole conker and needed an emergency operation at a cost of £280 to remove it.........

Bella the Bionic Dog

Taking out insurance on Bella turned out to be a wise move by her family for shortly after the policy became effective, an accident involving a shopping trolley, a wasp and a Vauxhall Cavalier left the unfortunate mutt with a broken back.

NAME	Bella
AGE	10 years
BREED	Cocker Spaniel
OWNER	Gillian Green

It was touch and go for some time but following surgery to erect some 'state of the art scaffolding' around her rear end, the dog was soon on her paws again and within a few weeks, back to waddling around the neighbourhood.

She quickly became known as 'The Bionic Dog' but happily, before the name could stick, Bella's back had knitted together nicely and the scaffolding was quickly dismantled. She's since made a complete recovery.

Don't Leave Me!

 Up until he was 18 months old, Bruno had led a very sad life locked away in a basement room where he'd been beaten, starved and generally abused.

Thankfully he was rescued and taken to a new home where he settled very quickly but since he'd never been allowed to socialise there was a giant kink in his character. He absolutely refused to leave his new owners' side.

He followed them everywhere and over the weeks he even developed a novel way of preventing them from leaving the house. As the hats and coats went on, Bruno wrapped his paws around their ankles and held on desperately as he was dragged across the carpet towards the front door. This surely was true love!

NAME	Bruno
AGE	4 years
BREED	Boxer
OWNER	Mrs C Cook

........When Honey, a
4-year-old Labrador
escaped from the garden
and was hit by a car, she
sustained only minor
injuries but the car cost
£492 to repair.........

Paddy's Happy Accident

Maybe it was because he had three extra toes on one foot that the other cats on the block had shunned Paddy and turned him into a bit of a loner. Trundling around his patch one day he was in collision with a car and on arrival at the vets it was found the only damage inflicted had been to his multi-toed foot.

The three extra digits were removed in a flash and the foot recovered to look like new. More importantly for the cat, when the wound had healed, it looked like everyone else's.

Paddy is now flavour of the month amongst the other neighbourhood mogs, which goes to prove that a few spare parts can come in very useful at times.

HERE COMES PADDY!

Mutley's Delight

Mutley was a dog with expensive tastes as he demonstrated one morning when he ate his owner's diamond earrings for breakfast!

A circle of interested parties, including 'the man from the Pru', surrounded the dog for a couple of days, willing him to return the sparklers by natural methods but Mutley showed no signs of giving up the treasure. After a long wait, his owner reluctantly gave permission for surgical removal of the gems and the operation was carried out successfully, and the earrings retrieved.

After all, as she explained to Mutley as he came round from the anaesthetic, a dog is a good mate but diamonds are a girl's best friend!

NAME	Mutley
AGE	2 years
BREED	Collie Cross
OWNER	Gill Powell

A VET'S STORY

The Headless Hamster

A client arrived at the consulting room with a hamster that had fallen off a table. The vet diagnosed shock and as he began treatment, the client asked if she could leave the furry bundle at the surgery while she went shopping.

The hamster was left to wait for her in a shoe box on the front desk but as the receptionist, in whose care it had been left returned from answering a call, she saw the practice cat skillfully removing the rodent from the box and legging it through an open window. He returned ten minutes later and presented her with the animal, minus its head!

When the client returned, the vets circled the wagons and told her that Cuddles had died of shock. This wasn't too far from the truth and to everyone's relief she didn't ask to see the body.

Alex Gets the Raspberry

When Alex the Setter returned from his summer holiday, his breath was so appalling he quickly became known around the neighbourhood as 'The Halitosis Kid!' His owner tried cleaning the dog's teeth and applying various homoeopathic remedies in an attempt to make the dog less antisocial, but in spite of these efforts, Alex could still fell a man at fifty paces.

A brave vet investigated the interior of the dog's mouth and after poking around for as long as he could hold his nose he retrieved a two-inch-long piece of raspberry cane that had been lodged in the back teeth for at least two weeks! The stick was removed and in no time it was safe once again to give Alex a kiss.

NAME	Alex
AGE	2 years
BREED	English Setter
OWNER	Mrs Sally Morley

Shabby Tabby

Some cats are born with a silver spoon but Tyler the tabby got off to the worst possible start in life. He was found by dustmen at the bottom of a rubbish chute.

Very skinny and covered in various bits of household waste, he was dropped off at the local veterinary practice where he was instantly adopted by a nurse.

Tyler is now very fat, very clean and very happy!

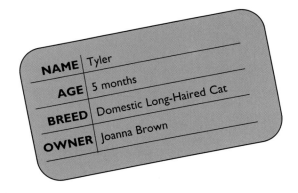

NAME	Tyler
AGE	5 months
BREED	Domestic Long-Haired Cat
OWNER	Joanna Brown

Dog Saves Snail in Burglary Drama

Cosi's owner had bought the Boxer to guard her London bedsit against intruders. One night at 2 am, the nightmare happened and she awoke to find the neighbourhood low life at the foot of the bed, relieving her of the few goodies she possessed. Cosi was snoring peacefully at her feet.

As she sat up in bed, the startled villain legged it for the door but half way there he trod on Brian, a large, yellow squeaking snail that was very close to Cosi's heart.

The dog was up in one bound. He lunged across the room, grabbed the snail and as the burglar disappeared through the window, went back to his rug, yawned, curled up and went back to sleep!

NAME	Cosi
AGE	7 years
BREED	Boxer
OWNER	A Sewell

Canine KO'd

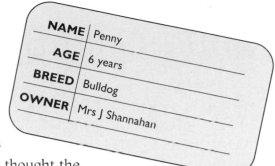

NAME	Penny
AGE	6 years
BREED	Bulldog
OWNER	Mrs J Shannahan

As ferocious as Penny the heavyweight Bulldog looked, when push came to shove she was no match for a tiny featherweight moggy who mistakenly thought the dog was threatening her kittens.

The cat went for a quick K.O. as Penny lumbered towards her brood and two lightening fast jabs and a vicious upper-cut later saw Penny sprawled on the kitchen floor.

The referee, who was cooking break-fast at the time, intervened quickly to save the dog from further punishment and he declared the mog winner by a technical knock out.

Penny suffered severe damage to her right eye which required urgent medical attention and she's since retired from the ring.

Solid Gold Spaniel

 A Cocker Spaniel, owned by a lady who worked in a jewelry shop, would often sit quietly under a table in a back office while his owner worked.

One day she was called to the front counter to serve and on her way upset a box of price tags, some of which the dog made a meal of in her absence.

That evening, as the Cocker relieved himself in the local park she was amused to see a small ticket sitting on top of his little gift which stated that it was 9 carat gold and could be bought for fourteen pounds!

........Toby the Rottweiler,
who is 6 years old and all of
nine stone, was attacked by
a Pug whilst out walking
with his owner. Toby ended
up with a visit to the vet for
tooth puncture wounds.........

SOLID
GOLD

A VET'S STORY

Tom's Treasure

Last year a Worcestershire vet encountered a very strange tom cat.
The cat lived in a large home with an orchard at the bottom of the garden.

Every Autumn the mog would wait for the crab apples to fall. As soon as this happened he'd methodically pick them up one by one and carry them to the front lawn where he'd construct a huge pyramid-like pile. Then, when he was satisfied with the size and shape of his creation, he'd climb to the top and lie around for hours on end dreaming and growling gently to himself.

The cat still waits every year for Autumn to come around and nobody as yet has been able to explain his strange behaviour.

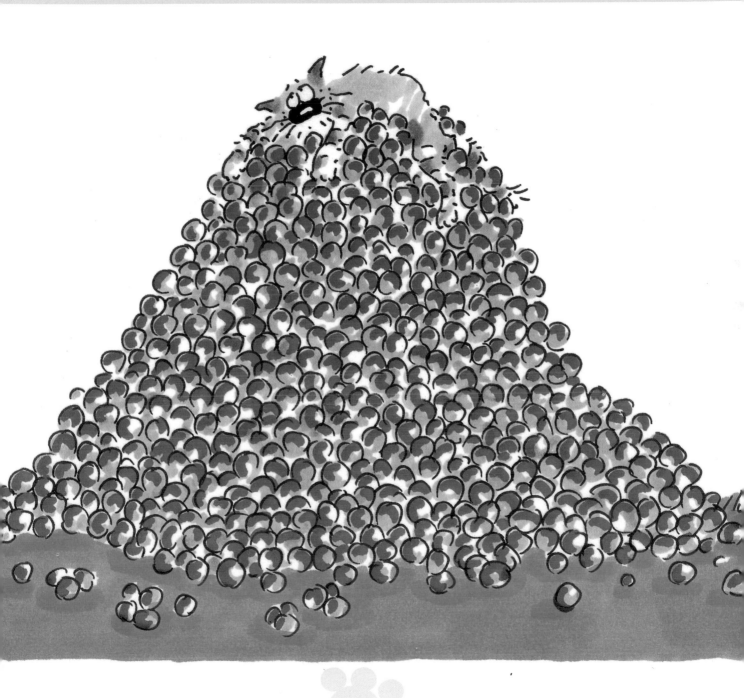

Snoopy Takes a Fall

With the exception of Zak on page 22 there are very few dogs around who can read, a skill that would have come in very useful for Snoopy the Poodle one morning during her usual walk to the ocean.

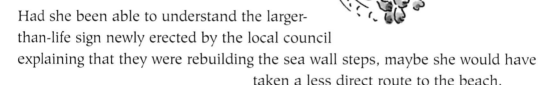

Had she been able to understand the larger-than-life sign newly erected by the local council explaining that they were rebuilding the sea wall steps, maybe she would have taken a less direct route to the beach.

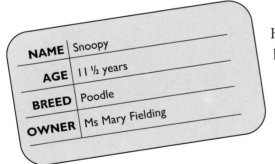

Her nose-first plummet onto the rocks below was spectacular but apart from severely dented pride Snoopy escaped with only minor damage.

NAME	Snoopy
AGE	11 ½ years
BREED	Poodle
OWNER	Ms Mary Fielding

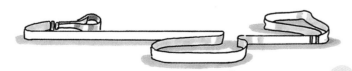

A VET'S STORY) Party Time

A seven-month-old moggy with a reputation for being something of a party goer was presented to his vet with a short length of tinsel protruding from his bottom!

Although everyone agreed it was a very smart bit of kit, it had to go and during surgery a piece of the stuff over two feet long was removed from the cat's gut!

Treacle's Sticky End

Although Treacle was a good all-round athlete with lots of stamina he had absolutely no navigational skills whatsoever. Out on the beach one morning attempting a new land speed record it was obvious to a crowd of onlookers that he was on collision course with a German Shepherd running in the opposite direction. The crowd was hushed as the two dogs closed.

NAME	Treacle
AGE	18 months
BREED	Whippet
OWNER	Miss S D Daniels
AMOUNT CLAIMED	Over £900 during his short life

At the last minute the German Shep tried to avoid the inevitable but it was too late. Treacle hit him head on at full speed, somersaulted into the air and landed in a heap on the sand with a broken bone in his neck.

Following treatment he made a good recovery and went on to have many narrow escapes whilst chasing rabbits and pheasants but sadly, some months later Treacle was killed when he collided head on with a car.

Balti Blaster

Gunther hit the bin sniffers' jackpot one day when he came across a baked potato discarded by his owner. Unfortunately for the dog the spud was filled with vindaloo curry and since anything he scavenged went straight down without touching the sides it was a few minutes before he realized his mistake.

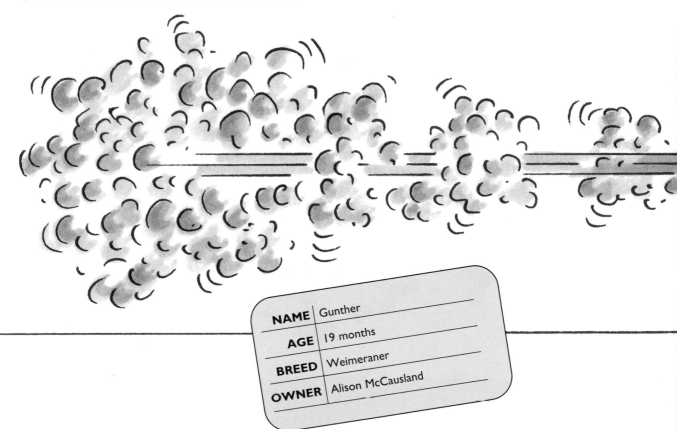

NAME	Gunther
AGE	19 months
BREED	Weimeraner
OWNER	Alison McCausland

It wasn't long before Gunther was suffering from 'Saturday Night Fever', that syndrome so well known to lager drinkers and when some of the vindaloo found its way into his eyes, it was realized the dog was in serious trouble.

Fortunately there was no lasting damage and following a visit to the vet and a sleepless night, Gunther recovered well.

His owner reports that the dog is now a far more selective bin sniffer!

Dicing With Death

It would be an understatement to say that Sinbad's medical background has been a complete disaster and his owners were truly thankful they'd had the foresight to have him fully insured.

Included among Sinbad's many brushes with death were a major eye operation, a crippling bout of eczema, an attack by a bitter and twisted Rottweiler who almost relieved him of an ear, a 50 feet plunge over a Cornish cliff which left him with fractured vertebrae and damaged spinal discs and a serious case of bloat that required major surgery on his internal plumbing.

Sinbad is now in his twelfth painful year and although he's now said by his owners to be in rude health they always keep his insurance policy where it can easily be found!

NAME	Sinbad
AGE	12 years
BREED	Chow Chow
OWNER	Mrs Rosemarie de Boyer
AMOUNT CLAIMED	£428.14 (total claims to date)

Tail End...

If you would like any more information about Pet Plan and its

services, The Pet Plan Charitable Trust, or if you'd simply like to send some of your humorous

cat and dog stories to us,

call us on

    tel. 0181 580 8080

    fax. 0181 580 8081

and ask for the Pet Plan

Press Department.

Or write to us at

    Press Department
    Pet Plan Group Ltd
    West Cross House
    2 West Cross Way
    Brentford
    Middx
    TW8 9DX